Red Canyon
Falling on Churches

Red Canyon
Falling on Churches

POEMAS, MYTHOS, CUENTOS

OF THE SOUTHWEST

Juliana Aragón Fatula

CONUN
DRUM
PRESS

A Division of Samizdat Publishing Group

CONUN
DRUM
PRESS

CONUNDRUM PRESS A Division of Samizdat Publishing Group.
PO Box 1279, Golden, Colorado 80402

For information, email INFO@CONUNDRUM-PRESS.COM.

ISBN: 978-1-942280-23-1

Library of Congress Control Number: 2015931182

Conundrum Press books may be purchased with bulk discounts for
educational, business, or sales promotional use. For information
please email: INFO@CONUNDRUM-PRESS.COM

Conundrum Press online: CONUNDRUM-PRESS.COM

Dedicated to my husband,
Vincent "Vinny" Fatula.
The love of my life, best-friend,
partner, esposo, soul-mate.
I asked la virgen de Guadalupe
for a good man and
la virgen sent me you.

"*A woman of color who writes poetry or paints or dances or makes movies knows there is no escape from race or gender when she is writing or painting. She can't take off her color and sex and leave them at the door . . . nor can she leave behind her history. Art is about identity, among other things, and her creativity is political . . . creative acts are forms of political activism.*"

—Gloria Anzaldúa, *Making Face, Making Soul Hacienda Caras*

Acknowledgments

My first thank you goes to my husband, Vincent, and my son, Daniel, for giving me a room of my own; and especially Dr. Judy Noel for giving me a room of my own in Pueblo, Colorado; Jerry Krale for giving me a room at Dillon Beach, California; Caleb Seeling and Sonya Unrein my publisher and editor at Conundrum Press; Kyle Laws, publisher Casa de Cinco Hermanas Press; mi hermano, Steve A. Aragón; my sisters and brothers from different mothers who have given me their encouragement in big and little ways: Aimeé Medina Carr, María Melendez Kelson, Juan Morales, Iver Arnegard, Tracy Harmon, and Leslie Fitzgerald. Also, my writing groups: the Macondistas, especially Jessica Helen Lopez, Natalia Trevino and Pat Alderete, mi East Los amiga; The Sexy Bitches, The Goatheads, and friends at Latino Writers Collective, Letras Latinas Institute for Latino Studies, writers: Linda Rodriguez, Xanath Caraza, Francisco Aragón, Adela Najarro, Manuel Ramos, Mario Acevedo, Tim Z. Hernandez; Colorado State University-Pueblo Southern Colorado Readings Series, *Pilgrimage Magazine*, Pueblo Community College, Rawlings Public Library, Pueblo School for Arts and Science. Colorado Humanities and the Center for the Book, thank you for making my dreams a reality.

And especially I thank my mentor, Sandra Cisneros, for encouraging me to apply to the Macondo Foundation for membership. The mission statement: "a community of poets, novelists, journalists, performance artists, and creative writers of all genres whose work is socially engaged. Their work and talents are part of a larger task of community-building and non-violent social change and their commitment to work for under-served communities through their writing."

I applied and received acceptance to attend my first Macondo Writer's Workshop in San Antonio, Texas. I checked into my dorm room at Our Lady of the Lake University and unpacked. While I was washing my hands, a thief entered my room and swept up my wallet, money, credit cards, identification, laptop, cell phone, and speakers. I heard a terrible crash outside the bathroom; I ran down the hall and saw no one anywhere. I filed a police report and caused quite a disturbance in the hallway with the excitement of being interviewed by the San Antonio police. I met most of the Macondistas in the hallway in the dorm and explained what happened. Every day during the workshops, I was introduced to writers as the one who was robbed in the dorms. I was definitely memorable.

Sandra heard of my robbery and how I lost all my money, credit cards, and laptop. The first thing she asked was if I was okay. The second question was if my manuscript had been stolen. No, it had not been stolen; I had a thumb drive in my pocket with all of my manuscripts. Sandra asked the Macondistas to help me with meals and to make sure my first visit was a good one. At the end of the week, Sandra held an auction and put up her costume from the public reading; she came as Glenda the Good Witch, complete with wand and crown. She managed to raise enough money to purchase a new laptop and gave me some spending money. She took care of me and made sure I left with a good experience.

When I went to the airport and was asked for identification by the TSA, I gave them the police report explaining that I'd been robbed. The agent asked if I had anything with my name and photo. I had saved one copy of my book for the trip home.

I showed it to the agent and he smiled and said, "That's pretty cool!" I made literary history by being allowed to use my book cover for my identification to pass security at an international airport. I left with more than the experience of being robbed. I was given so much from the community of writers I met at Macondo. I am no longer a Mocosa; I am now a Macondista. Since then, my writing and confidence have excelled. The opportunity to meet Sandra was life changing for me. Her encouragement has been invaluable and her friendship priceless. Now it's my opportunity to do the same for new writers who are socially engaged, creating community-building and non-violent social change.

Some of these poems appeared in *The Road I Ride Bleeds,* published in issue four of Casa de Cinco Hermanas Press, Pueblo, CO, 2012: "Parable," "My Homegirl Don't Eat Pork," "Blue-eyed Tattooed," "You Just Had To Be An Indian, Didn't You?," "The River," "Ehecatl god of Wind," "Red Canyon Falling On Churches," "Estrellas," "goddess," "Nopal Song," "Hanging From The Hood," "How Women Created Men," "Pobrecita," and in earlier versions in *Hispanic Cultural Experience* 2010-11 and 2011-12, anthologies of Colorado State University-Pueblo: "How Women Created Men," "My Homegirl Don't Eat Pork," and "Parable."

Preface

Náhuatl, language of the Aztecs, and Spanglish, language of the Chicano, flows like a river through the poems and stories. A tortilla is not bread; it is a tortilla.

Curenderas—healers—cure the sick and cursed.

Los muertos dance bum da da bum, in the graveyard.

Mystical desert creatures trick the coyote as they cross the border.

Creation stories reveal myths woven from feminism and rock'n'roll lava.

Magic and spirituality blend into the anguish of addiction.

There are no victims, only survivors: women who make scholarship money by selling tamales. Mothers who love unconditionally their children of the sun.

The nueva Chicana's cuentos y poemas teach forgiveness and healing through tears and laughter.

Sacredness of stones reminds us how everything on Earth is holy.

Contents

Pobrecita

sis's bare walls,
the shriveled avocado in the cocina.
the death of my sister worse than the death of my mother.
what if I had been her, born in the forties instead of the fifties
only la frontera and fear?
sister always carried her ID
even though she was born here.
I carry my shame
of being a pocha,
what if sister had gone to college instead of me?

sister bought me gifts at the dollar store,
never asked for anything from me,
worked three jobs, came home tired, pobrecita,
watched CNN—listened to stories
about uneducated, undocumented, uninsured.

. . . survivor guilt crazy.
at home, my iPad, iPhone, feng shui,
Anaya, Cisneros on my Kindle.
Frida and Diego on my warm terra-cotta walls;
feather bed overrun with pillows.
I flip Freddy Fender on the iPod and sing,
"Wasted days and wasted nights."
Pobrecita, it was one of her favorites.

my fear, five siblings to bury,
no healthcare, no insurance,
no satin liner savings.
someone has to be the last one to die.
out of respect,
I owe my family this.

someone has to water
the heirloom philodendron,
pack the apron stained with love,
dishes chipped but lovely,
quilt tied with faded yarn,
chili ristra on the porch,
vase filled with sugarless candy—
hidden under the bed, the good stuff . . .
Twinkies and Ho Hos, secrets of diabetes.

Dance to Death

dios, let me dance
my way out.
dance to death!
doña Sebatiana will
transport me in her
carreta de la muerta
to the dark world.
if laughter is the best medicine,
dancing is the cure.

Slow Down Dance

ninety in a fifty
down the valley
the red river curves
uphill
skids down
stops at the beach
where fish
jump jump jump
moon dance
all night long

Love Lies Bleeding

Lo mío, mío y lo tuyo también mío.
What's mine is mine and what's yours is also mine.

My love, loves bleeding, bleeding.
I let *you* out once.
You ripped the night, pursued
dark eyes and ice smiles,
searched for that purrfect pet,
settled for a cougar
wearing a halter top
and Jimmy Choos.
Her pussy-pie-face
melted you
like manteca.
My love, loves bleeding, bleeding.

December-May romance.
I loved you like
a red hot poker in the eye,
like a hot air balloon in a hurricane,
like hunger eats a cheeseburger,
like a radio in the bathtub,
like a foot in a bear trap . . .
My love, loves bleeding, bleeding.

The Cage

Cat stalks the birds and bugs
like a hit man,
cries to kick-it with other felines.
The dangers, the wild.
I lock her up in the house.
A predator, you know?

The cat naps,
tires of the bird
that waves in and out of sight.

Hungry for the hunt,
fat with content,
yellow bird tries to drink nectar
but lacks the proper beak.
Soars away desperate
for something sweet to eat.

Nopal Song

Tío told me to eat cactus
for my diabetes,
his eighty-seven-years
stretched before me
on twisted bones,
weathered soul.

His laugh raised tears
and memories
of sitting 'round the
kitchen table Mom, Dad,
tía and tío.
Young and spirited
drinking with Hank Williams'
"Cheatin' Heart"
and "Walkin' After Midnight"
with Patsy Cline.

They were selling tamales
for scholarships,
building dreams out of masa.

Red Chile Ristra

supple sweet chile
ristra cherry blaze
dries in my doorway
brings good fortune
reminds me why my
dreams come in Spanish

The Shit You Pulled After You Were Dead

I walk up the hill to visit,
change the flowers on your grave,
pull weeds, dust off the headstone.

When you were alive you slapped
every one of my boyfriends in the face, hard . . .
You'd get shit-faced and slap, slap, slap . . .
You must'a slapped twenty men in your heyday . . .

My boyfriends always laughed
as they rubbed pain away and asked,
"What the hell?"
I watched you do it for years
and started warning my boyfriends,
"Hey, my mom's gonna slap you sometime
really fuckin' hard, wachale."
It was your thing.
You never slapped my husband.
I guess it was just a boyfriend slap . . .
You never slapped me . . .
What were you testing?

Did you want to piss them off
to see if they'd punch you in the face
like your ex-husband used to do?
Is that why your nose was broken?

Did he destroy your beauty
like a storm breaks the dam?
You said you'd never
forgive anyone who hurt you . . .

Are you in heaven or hell,
wrestling with forgiveness
for those assholes
slapping the shit
out of them?

When I threw the first shovel
of dirt on your coffin,
I leaned over and my sunglasses
slid down the six-foot hole.
I crawled in the grave with you
and fished them out.
You playing tricks . . .

The night I spent with you in the ER,
watched you depart,
you squeezed my hand
and wouldn't let go,
your eyes wide, mouth twisted.
Did you see demons?
Was Grandma's hell and brimstone
waiting for you like a hole
you couldn't crawl out of?
What were you so afraid of, Mom?

Dead or alive,
you are the best
part of me.
When I miss you,
I just look in the mirror.
I smile because
I don't care that you got drunk
and slapped my boyfriends;
they had it coming.

The River

Remember crying yourself to sleep
when Mom didn't come home
on Christmas Eve?
Her mestiza nose,
diamond iris eyes,
red, red wine lipstick,
her ratty hair;
Mom dressed in stilettos,
her black leather jacket
with the big belt.

Her evil-honey voice
screaming with the radio,
"What ya gonna' do
when ya get outa' jail?
I'm gonna have some fun!"
A bottle of Bud between her legs,
cigarette smoke filling the car,
her passed out behind the wheel,
parked at The Bird Club.
Where did we hide
when she came home borracho
and whipped us for daring
to take her young ones
to swim in the river;
the river witch
waiting to drown us;
Mom waiting for us
to come out from
under the bed?

Un gato viejo, ratón tierno;
the cocoman is an old man
who likes young girls,"
Mom told us every night—

I was ten, running wild
through Duck Park,
across the train tracks,
under Black Bridge,
in the horse field,
no longer afraid
of the cocoman.
I was never as afraid
of the cocoman
as I was of Mom's wrath,
the crosses on the back of my thighs,
the belt buckle marks on my legs . . . still.

Fetish

I wasn't always a mestiza diva;
I was plain and simple.
Twice I tried to bake and knit.
Three times I married.
Once, I fell in love.

I dreamt of sex with shiny
black-haired japonéses
with perfect complexions.
The japonés looked like Chicanos
with exotic eyes.

In my hometown, all the Chicanos
were my cousins.
So I married a white man.
I served tea on my geisha knees—
I wore the kimono, played the docile girl.

It felt good to take my life,
to sacrifice like a samurái
rather than live in shame.

Estrellas

Estrellas fall up toward morning,
scented of jasmine June.
Tang of time comes into bud,
soft stone glistens,
blue-black hatchling cries,
calling the night.
Listen.

Frida

God cast perfect light,
oozed violence high in the tree top.
En casa azul,
Frida captured hews of mist,
web of pain,
harsh beauty of ruin,
Zen of calla lilly
and violet.
Resentful,
the copper nightingale
refused to sing.

Desert Creatures with Insomnia
Waited for Night

They can see in the dark,
don't need night vision goggles;
they like to wear them anyway,
because they look so cool.

The trickster falls asleep,
the crazy creatures
tiptoe into the coyote's den
and steal all of his stash:
his Snickers, Cheetos,
Bengay, Prozac,
Ambien, and TV remote.

This is why
the coyote howls
at the moon at night.

Desert Creatures Trek Across
Tuscon, Arizona

Ay! Don't forget your pinche passports, pendejos!

* In response to the assault on Mexican American Studies curricula,
including primary source literature, in the Tuscon school system.

Parable

El coyote, pendejo, wore a pistola,
Para qué todos would know who was boss.
He stumbled, stumbled, crawled
dizzy with wine,
forgot to howl at the moon.

The desert creatures huddled
under the nopal scheming
por la noche. Las criaturas
prepared la luna loca de masa.
Their battered lil' hands pounded out the maíz.
Shards of blistered skin bled on the tortilla
and stained the face crimson.

El coyote dreamt
of Hollywood hot tubs,
woke from his stoned torpor,
grabbed the bloody moon.
He kneaded the tortilla into a woman
with olive colored eyes
and lugged
her off to his cave. The desertó creaturas
laughed at the fool with his masa wife,
heard el cabrón howl all night.

My Homegirl Don't Eat Pork

Panza llena, corazón contento.
A full belly, a happy heart.

Candie and I have chai latte,
argue about tamales.
I use la manteca y los chicharrones.
She uses orgánico chicken and olive oil.

Mine es finger frickin' lickin';
her's is kinda' stickin'
like caca in your chonies.

Mine are tasty y caliente;
her's are not even tempting.
No chicharrones, no manteca,
no chile verde con marón,
cochina, pero
she wants me
to give her my recipes.

I tell her, hijita,
real mexicanos
don't cook with olive oil,
whole wheat, organic chicken!

Pero, because I love the challenge,
I drag out the tamal pan—
you know the big ass one
you have to store in the garaje
cuz' it's so fruckin' huge
and your cocina
is so pinche small, enit?

I take mí gringa loca,
Candie, shopping.

I pass by the pork
por de la chingada chicken
and grow sad, lo siento.
Then comes the choice,
instant or old school masa harina.
Instant? You sure?

I reach for the lard and Candie
gives me the evil eye.
So, I settle for shortening.
Spice aisle, ah!
Orégano, comino,
garlic, chile pequeño!!!!
And she says,
"Not too hot or spicy."
And I'm like WTF!
For reals?

I move onto the hojas
and reminisce:
Mom and Dad
used to drive to Florence
in their '67 Chevy
to visit their friend, Corn,
to buy his hojas—
he grew the best maíz
in the county.
His husks had sabor!

My hojas soak in the sink;
Candie steams her's
like a freak.
I know, huh?
Simón!
Mamás tamales
a two hundred
year-old recipe.

Órale!
They'd slaughter a pig
and make chicharrones
and lard from the drippings—
grew their own chile, comino
and ground their corn
into harina
in the molcajete
made of lava stone;
they roasted that meat
until it fell off the bone—
la familia toda would
shred the meat
and spread the masa
on the hojas.

The kitchen aroma
knocked you out;
it was so spicy! Caliente!
Neighbors showed up—
relatives came out
of the woodwork—
outlaws came out
of whatever hole
they were hiding in—
la música began
and before you knew it—
you had una fiesta!

The beer cans popped,
tequila spilled—
everyone
ate-drank-sang-danced
and praised the cooks!
Everyone knew
the tamales had lard

and didn't give a pinche
chingón!
"Orgánico" tamales
taste like caca.

The next day
we would scream
for ice cream,
steam came
out our culos,
our heads were pounding
from the tequila,
the butt was on fire,
and still . . .
we had tamales
and cervezas
for breakfast.

Poema for Sandra Cisneros

Whenever I can't sleep, I pretend I'm in the house on Mango Street, casa azul. You're there in the kitchen sloshing a drink all over your slippers. You wink and the corner of your mouth rides up like, 'waz up?'

If you lived in my hometown, you'd have coffee on the back porch with me and we'd share secrets. I'd pop in sometimes to your house on Banana Street and we'd try on each other's clothes. You are the sister I never got because my parents were too busy having babies in Colorado and you were born in Chicago.

You can't sleep tonight either. You are probably in your big fat chair sipping coffee and thinking about the poem I wrote for you. The coffee tastes like whipped cream with a splash of cinnamon. It takes on the flavor of the mountains and waterfalls, down smooth.

If you lived here we'd meet at the river-walk and ride our fat tire bikes up and down in the dark. That damn moon is so full it overflows and we could put our mouths underneath and catch some moon juice. It's quiet there at night except for the occasional mountain lion and black bear, but they mind their own business. We could stop, sit on the park bench and watch the night flow down to Pueblo. I'd tell you about the time I read your book and cried because I never knew there was an Esperanza in me. I'd ask you why women aren't supposed to be loose, drink alone, puff on cigars and cuss. You'd laugh and say, *this is just a dream, wake up, pendeja.*

How Women Created Men

Dark-skinned women
with amber eyes were the first.
Mujeres dreamt of men
and built them out of clay and twigs,
los hombres bonitos
smelled like earth.
They resisted mujeres chichis
as long as they could,
until por la noche,
toda la gente plunged into lust.

Body heat melted rocks
turned flesh and bones into lava.
The ground shook and rocked;
large manzanas toppled from trees.
The serpent was knocked senseless;
the women laughed until they peed.

Azteca Grain

Slabs of stone line the garden
tendrils hang heavy
ready to turn—
seeds drop
low, low, low
clusters pull the plant
onto its bloody bursting head
shears sharpened sit in lull
while amaranth,
Azteca grain,
grows lush.

Tenochtitlan

blue-raven hair,
draped in wicked darkness,
her face absent lips or eyes,
she feels her way—
the wind carries la bruja
in the river mist.

she searches in torment for her niños,
but they were lost
five hundred years ago
in Tenochtitlan.

the river witch grieves their watery grave;
wails for children
to replace the ones she drowned—
she floats like fog, vanishes,
dragged into the thin dim dawn.

Smell of the Devil

La noche es capa de pecadores.
Night is the cover of the sinner.

Darker than the void—
the cocoman's shiny,
sharp teeth,
his hair hangs wooly.
He sheds his face—
charcoal flesh
crisps from skeletal bones.
His scream shrills
deep from his bowels,
gurgles in his throat.
You accept the dare—
alone at dusk,
you follow
smothering stare,
his devil stench—
sour wine; ripe, rank, rancid
searing wind ignites the grass—
the cocoman inhales the smoke—
blows rings
above his gangrenous head—
veils his ominous shadow
of tarántula legs
sneak footsteps,
slogs his nails in the dirt,
slices open the earth—
the green stemmed circle of light
wisps you away,
thick as heat,
coiled in the black
cleft of night.

Goddess

me, a girl in a viejita's body.
a crooked tooth smile, sagging eyelids
flirting with men half my age.
it's scandalous, I torture them:
built like a brick shit house—stacked,
chocolate kiss nipples—legs tight, lean,
the cant soft, like calabacitas
tender and unripened en mi milpa.

Recipe For Fever

soak potatoes sliced thin in vinegar
place on patient's forehead
(or is it the feet? that's what they do in el valle)
wrap in a clean, white, linen headband
replace with new potatoes every so often
keep patient in bed
pray until fever breaks

Nature's Poison

La bruja collects
devil's claw, narcissus,
dragon tail,
hemlock, beaver poison,
snakeroot, ghostweed,
belladona, bloodroot,
death camus, yew,
and deadly nightshade.
From tree to bush to river bank,
the witch scours the region
in search of lethal tea.

The sun appears,
the dark one vanishes like a myth,
the victim never knows he is doomed—
he senses an evil eye
staring at the back of his cabeza.
Sometimes the stench of rot
permeates the blackness
and a heavy hand
holds him powerless to flee.

Death strikes—
the witch dances and sings
around the cauldron, the flames.
The dying chokes on his tea,
whispers the name
of the one who wishes him dead—
but no one can prove the culprit guilty—
that mystery fades
into witchy history.

Nunca, Nunca Give a Pregnant Woman

mistletoe, tansy, morning glory,
mandrake, locoweed, foxglove,
or oleander.

Just ask my tía,
she'll tell you
about the time
she got pregnant
and had an abortion
the old-school way.

La curandera mixed herbs,
dried seeds,
flower petals,
bark, weeds,
and blood from her fingertip.
"Just for color," she smirked.

La curandera told her,
"There are two kinds:
therapeutic abortion or habitual.
Some women," she claimed,
"don't practice birth control;
instead they just abort.
Those are the truly evil women,"
she told tía.

She named the village women
who she deemed habitual.
She confessed to dream
of poisoning these women,
"Just a taste of juice,
that will surely kill them.
It only takes twelve leaves,"
she brags "and twenty-four hours."

She asked tía what kind of miscarriage
she desired. Tía smiled and whispered,
"The holy abortion."

Then la curandera prayed to Tonantzin
the goddess of women
who died in childbirth;
she prayed for the soul of the unborn;
held out her hand for the ten dollars,
danced in a circle in her little moccasins.

Mal de Ojo

A childless woman can give the evil eye,
not to be evil,
if she looks at a baby or small child with
envy in her heart.
But the child suffers
from dehydration and withers.

Alma knew a child so beautiful
that his mother had to warn women
not to look at him with envy.

An amulet bracelet
with an eye painted on it
can be worn by the child
for protection.

A person wearing something
that might cause you to be filled with envy
should ask you to touch the item
to dispel the envy/evil.

Alma's mother always caressed
her daughter's clothing that she liked.
"I'm seeing with my fingers
instead of my eyes," she'd say.

Alma would touch the hem
of her friends' children's shirts.
She didn't want to curse her friends' kids,
so she pulled their clothes
as they walked by her.

Lightly sweep an egg
over the patient's body
to absorb the evil eye power.

Break open the egg
in a clean glass
filled with cold water.

The shape of an egg like an eye
indicates mal de ojo,
or a black spot on the egg,
means someone has envy
or is jealous of the patient.

Cover the bowl and egg
with a straw or palm,
place under patient's head,
or pass the egg over the body
in a cross pattern
and recite the Lord's Prayer.
Our father who art in heaven . . .

Let the patient
sleep with the egg
under their pillow
and continue to pray.

***

Alma's parents drank
every weekend.
They partied like rockstars.
The children were never
neglected
nor hungry,
but still
they all grew up

addicted
to something:
drugs,
booze,
food,
love . . .

Alma remembers
her parents drank
because their parents drank,
and they drank
because their parents drank . . .

Alma collected her teardrops in a jar.
She labeled the tears: ALMA'S TEARS.
As she grew older, she filled many jars.
Her jars lined the windowsill.
She laughed into the jars as she tightened the lids.

Hanging from the Hood

father holding onto a lantern
hanging from the hood
of a Model T Ford
twenty miles per hour
on the dirt road
from New México to Colorado
in the dark summer night
stars bouncing up above

no moon to light the way
praying for land, water, sun
leaving grandfather
with his herd of sheep
grandmother with her garden

father searching for generosity,
hoping for prosperity
longing for equality
finding only
stars bouncing up above.

Toci

Aztecas worshipped Toci during harvest season, sacrificing a young girl, the daughter of a local ruler who was destined to marry an Azteca chief, ripping out the young girl's heart and flaying her skin to be worn by a priest; so that she could become the goddess, Toci.
—*Náhuatl Myth*

Silently, Toci walks around el río
toward the purple mesa, her
head tilted to the side,
counting the children
in the sky—the ones
she could not save.

She burned out like a candle
inside out, slow, steady flame,
melted back into clay,
licked trees and tasted bark
when it rained.

No one can match her scars;
secrets stay with her.
She was quiet when she should be,
silent like the stars.

Coyolxauhqui and the Star Gods

Coyolxauhqui, feeling disgraced by her mother's immaculate conception, created a plot with the four hundred centzón huitznahuas to destroy her brother, Huitzilopochtli, while he was still in the womb.
—*Náhuatl Myth*

The night was mine;
centzón huitznahuas
shined just for me.
Mother, earth goddess—
Father, sun god.
Azteca princess,
they bowed when I entered.

Tonantzin betrayed us all.
Tricked and seduced
by the god
of immaculate conception,
her flaming feather
ball of lust.
Brought forth
the god of war;
his armor
turquoise and emerald.
My brothers and sisters
shamed by mother,
drew their obsidian knives,
baby in her womb.
Dug our own grave with disgust,
condemned, transformed
into the moon and stars
in the glittering world,
waiting for the new sun.

Cielo in Flux

I am Tonantzin—
the filth eater.
I erase sins,
eat the mierda,
make everyone clean.

I've taken everyone's
shit for years—Why not
get credit for it?
I am the mother
of the gods: my son,

Huitzilopochtli,
god of war, saved
me from mis niños,
busted my daughter into
pieces of the moon.
My four-hundred
children, now stars at
night, far from home,
always in my sight.

Tonantzin

Náhuatl, mother of the gods,
heart of the earth,
cover us with your tilma,
erase all of our sins,
grind bones into flour,
add Quetzalcóatl's blood,
leave the soul alone.
Create new people.
Born in the fifth world,
we are the children
of the sun.

When I Die

I want to be born again
this time as a healer –
instead of a wheeler and dealer.
I want to see the trees movin',
feel the earth groovin',
hear the ocean's tide purr,
smell the skin of the sea.
In my next life,
let me be a woman again.
Let me rip and bleed
and give birth.
I want to create
not destroy life.

Tezcatlipoca

The feathered serpent
stood in the dark,
mumbled wicked charms,
conjured the moon,
the god of smoke and lies,
and his obsidian mirror,
god of temptation and deceit,
seduced creación:
Quetzalcóatl, precioso twin,
drank pulque made of maguey.
Hexed, he raped his sister.
Drawn to Tezcatlipoca's
smoky mirror, al agua negra.
Quetzalcóatl's image reflected shame,
his suicide by funeral pyre.
From the flames flew birds,
carried his heart to the heavens
transformed into the morning star.

Chantico-Firebreather

Earth turns
to sparks
of fire storms,
floods and quakes.
Chantico snuffs
out the flames,
lures death
into the vault
of the sky,
consumes
all of man's
mistakes.

Ehecatl god of Wind

In the afternoon,
silence
pampas grass sways
el viento,
lullabies.
I forget to breath.
Mother Earth holds
me like a newborn child
—religiously.

Red Canyon Falling On Churches

Peach clouds drift,
darkling heavens
light as bone.

The road
I ride bleeds,
crickets scream.
The butterfly's wing
bitch-slaps my face,
with just a trace
of stardust.

Prayer floats
between cottonwoods
in the open peaks.
Chaos blooms
where secrets meet.

Clean For One Day

Lalo got clean one day,
saw the color of the world
wasn't technicolor.
His first time off the meth.
Mom had aged with long grey braids,
a crease between her brows.

In an old hippie dress
that made her look
like she rocked Woodstock,
she tiptoed barefoot,
limped a bit as she rose from the couch.

Lalo smelled his mom's
Juicy Fruit/chai breath.
She laughed long and hardy,
gave him a tight squeeze
around the ribs. Then she punched
him in the gut with her puny
fist. Lalo groaned;
it was their special sign.

He sat down at the table,
mom running to the cocina,
balancing tortillas and coffee,
spilling all the way.
Around the room,
crucifixes, altars with la virgen,
rosaries and saints.

He ate the tortilla, drank her coffee,
told his mom a funny story
about his indian name,
Two Left Feet Stumbles Along,
just to hear her laugh.

He kissed her goodbye
on the lips, looked her dead
in the eye and walked out the door.
He could still hear her
giggles as he dropped out of sight.

Inky Moon

Ten years grave digging under the inky moon,
haunted knots under sleeves of shame.
Mom hugged my bony frame,
looked into my candy-eyes,
saw Jesus and Mary.
I flaunted my track marks,
flinched as Mom blew like a tsunami,
drifted disjointed,
soft, out of the room.
I blinked hard,
slammed love
into my scabby vein.
"Merry fuckin' Christmas, Mom!"

Chimeric Moon

The sassy housewife drinks lilac tonic,
falls down the stairs, never spills a drop—

yaps and spins. Saturday night suicide note
acute and scissor sharp. Wax away

oh, chimeric moon,
attrition armored like fables—

the gods all agog, await
her grassy change, monstrous, to atone.

Trick of Moon

Burns the sky,
glares like god's angry eye . . .
rain rages in windows,
flows on the floor,
dirty drops and desire.
Sinvergüenza sparrow sent to smash
my shameful head and heart—
drink from me—
your first taste of smack.
Forgive me for being addicted to crack,
for being fifteen—scared;
forgive me,
'cuz it kind of hurts.
Selfish vata
wanting to have teenage fun,
forgetting to sacrifice,
living in the school bus,
in the cold, cold cave,
addicted to love;
forgive me,
'cuz it kind of hurts.
Prayers could not change me—
it took falling for you
to keep me from drowning.
Por las cochinas dudas—
these dirty doubts,
unworthy of devotion.

Blue-eyed Tattooed

Indian boy with a crew-cut,
I've got magic in my soul,
Mom only fifteen,
a Chiquita bonita.
A teenage girl, only a child,
dark eyed and wild.
Lucky, I was born on a blue moon.
I've got mojo from head to toe.
Mom's cooking beans in the cocina.
Daddy's in the head with his spoon.
He rarely sleeps at night,
ojos twinkling in the dark,
twisting, sneaking tight.

Coffee Out of Bark

Lie down with me, smell the stars,
reach out your crusty hand
look into the future
and see time.
Eat red roses, pretend it's steak,
drink from the ditch, shit in the alley.
Rise from your shopping cart, give me that ride
to Christianity. Stop at the Loaf-'N Jug,
grab sugar and cream.
We'll brew coffee out of bark,
use our love for cups.
Dream with me,
smoke this pipe,
sing that song I like
about the homies.
Dig your bed in the dirt,
use my shoulder for your pillow,
hug me 'til I puke.
Please be here
in the morning.

Guerrera

drinks to blindness,
rips the room apart in rage,
pulls and tears everything into rubble.
she sobers, returns to the room,
quietly sweeps with a broom
all that she has destroyed,
throws it away.
She sits in the middle of the room,
looks around at the emptiness.

The Mexican in Me

can't watch the news
gives me the pinche blues
jita goes to school
in east los
thinks she's cool

daddy works so frickin' hard
just so she can have a car
she's a vata loca
she's a runaway, pendeja

don't she see her daddy's breakin'
he's tired, he's crackin'
works too much, too long
never home, jita's always alone.

jita's sneakin' out the window
she's drinkin' down below
partying with her homies
she feels so very lonely.
daddy better watch out
jita's headed for a fall
bound to make that call,
"dad, I'm in jail
please, I need bail
daddy I need you."

jita's only fifteen
mama's a crack queen
aint got no mama no mo'
no role model
she just wants to be cool
so she ditches school

can't watch the news
just get the fuckin' blues
no news is good news
my mama used to say
don't say nothin'
if you got nothin' good to say

my mama taught me everything
'cept how to deal with this crack thing
guess I'll just hit the pipe
so much for this pinche life.
jita's gonna learn the hard way
just like her mama,
the crack queen of L.A.

You Just Had To Be An Indian,
   Didn't You?

Mom's long Medusa braids
like twisted fingers
pointing to the stars—
they're top heavy
as an ancient moon.

She's real,
like a drag queen's décor,
it hurts.
She's southwest
like Santa Fe cacti,
easy like an orchid
but we wear gloves
cuz' she's sharp as a razor.
When she drums at powwow,
it's like a bomb
dropped on your head—
her love long.
It's great-giant
Indian love.

Jesus' Runway

Clouds of magenta
casting scenes of god-like skies,
singing a death song to ancestors.
I dove into the calm glass.
The light of night rising
into a globe of lunar glow
a streak of shimmer
on the lake like a runway
for Jesus to walk on water.

Holy Bones

starless blue-black night,
la muerte dances on the grave.
not like the funky chicken dance,
more like the conga.
hips sway, the earth shakes,
the dance of the dead
down down down.

the bones *bang da da bang da da bang.*
el viento breezes through tired ribs.
more funny than scary.
muertos, juntos raíces,
get along when they're dead,
porque, las calaveras
are all the same color—bone.

They Only Eat Their Husbands

Love, Travel, and the Power of Running Away by Cara Lopez Lee

978-1-942280-00-2

In this adventure travel memoir, twenty-six-year-old Cara Lopez Lee runs away to Alaska after a lover threatens to kill her. There, she finds herself in a complicated love triangle. Nine years later, sick of love, she runs away again, this time to backpack alone around the world. *They Only Eat Their Husbands* is a memoir about this year-long trek through Thailand, China, Nepal, Spain, and Ireland, recounting with dazzling honesty and humor one woman's journey to self-discovery.

Crazy Chicana in Catholic City

Poems by Juliana Aragón Fatula

978-0-9713678-4-5

"These poems balance the raw honesty and rage at life's adversities with tenderness, humor, and healing. Whether it be through haunting characters like el Cucuy or la Llorona or the family members she honors, she unites a cast of compelling personas who show us teh everyday struggles we share and teach through their nature and complexitites." —Juan J. Morales